I
BELIEVE

COLIN DAY is one of the founders of the Jesus Centre in Birmingham. While working at the Centre he conceived the idea of presenting basic Christian truths in a way that is both informative and enjoyable to read. *I Believe* is the fruit of that idea.

I BELIEVE

Colin Day

FALCON BOOKS
EASTBOURNE

ISBN 0 86239 004 4

Illustrations based on ideas by Ray Price

Printed in Great Britain for
FALCON BOOKS – KINGSWAY PUBLICATIONS LTD
Lottbridge Drove, Eastbourne, E. Sussex BN23 6NT by
Richard Clay (The Chaucer Press) Ltd, Bungay, Suffolk.
Typesetting by Nuprint Services Ltd, Harpenden, Herts.

A few words to myself

How can I use this book? Well, apart from reading left to right, it's really up to me. If I wish I can start at the beginning and systematically work my way through the different sections. By the end I should have a clear understanding of what Christians believe and how those beliefs affect their lives.

But, I may prefer to dip at random into different parts of the book. That will be fine too, as the sections have all been written as self-contained units. So they will make sense in any order, big chunks or small.

If I am really enthusiastic I might even wish to use the text as a basis for Bible study. The relevant Bible verses are at the back of the book. There is no extra charge for using them.

Finally, I can use this brief outline either to gain a bird's eye view of Christian truths, or else as a launching pad for thinking more deeply on their implications for my life.

So the ball is in my court. I have before me a multi-purpose information pack. How I use it is entirely up to me.

I BELIEVE

in God, the Father almighty, creator of
heaven and earth.

I believe in Jesus Christ, his only Son,
our Lord.
He was conceived by the power of the
Holy Spirit
and born of the Virgin Mary.
He suffered under Pontius Pilate,
was crucified, died, and was buried.
He descended to the dead.
On the third day he rose again.
He ascended into heaven,
and is seated at the right hand
of the Father.
He will come again to judge the living
and the dead.

I believe in the Holy Spirit,
the holy catholic church,
the communion of saints,
the forgiveness of sins,
the resurrection of the body,
and the life everlasting.
Amen.

Ever since the resurrection of Christ his followers have found it helpful to bring together in a brief, yet thorough form the essentials of their beliefs. So over a period of time various creeds (which are statements of belief) have come into use. The early church used them as a basis of instruction for new Christians. Then, later on, they became incorporated into the worship of Christian groups.

The creed quoted at the front of this book is known as the Apostles' Creed. It was in use by the end of the fourth century A.D. and is still recited regularly in many churches today, in an act by which Christians affirm their basic beliefs—both as individuals and as a group.

The following pages attempt to draw out the nature of these beliefs and their implications for our daily lives.

I
BELIEVE

I BELIEVE . . .

To help our understanding of God the Bible provides us with a series of images, each one of which illustrates a different aspect of his character. God is portrayed as a King, a Father, a Shepherd and a Judge. The Bible makes no attempt to explain the origins of God. It simply states that he has always existed.

Before I can even begin to believe, I need to have some idea of what, or who, I am believing in. The Bible tells us that God—besides being Spirit, all-powerful, everlasting and unchanging—is also personal. This means he has a mind, emotions, values, and a sense of purpose.

* * * * * * *

Merely believing in something is not going to do me much good at all. Biblical belief—or faith—is characterized by action. It is not a mystical condition. It is my active response to the love and truth of the living God. It involves my deciding to trust him and follow him in a practical way. I must learn to obey God—that is how I will know and show that I really believe.

How do I obey God? By doing what I see him saying through the Bible, and by acting on what I sense him saying to me in prayer.

"Such a lovely sermon Vicar - but you didn't really mean **I** have to do anything about it, did you?"

Biblical faith involves a personal relationship. I place my trust in a living God, not a series of religious ideas. I need to be very careful not just to 'believe in' or 'agree with' God, but to act definitely on what I accept in my head and heart. It is as I transfer my belief from idle agreement into a distinct life-style that God will become real to me. When I do nothing I give God no opportunity (or need!) to move in my life.

* * * * * * *

The most obvious characteristic of my belief should be a regularly exercised trust in God. This trust ought to be practical and confident. It should see me through those times when God's way of living takes me in a different direction from that of the crowd. On such occasions my trust knows nothing of a slightly resentful 'grin and bear it' attitude, but is characterized by a sparkling enjoyment of the certainty that God reigns and is in full control.

My belief in God is meant to make me actively commit myself to him—to his values and his objectives. There is no place for stagnation in the life of a believer. I need to be available for service and willing to stand up and be counted as someone who is on the Lord's side. I need to get involved.

As my involvement increases and confidence in God deepens, so my faith will gradually become more of an attitude than a series of separate decisions. Trusting God will come naturally to me. I will see that it works!

* * * * * * *

Faith requires discipline. I must be single-minded in my determination to base my life day by day upon the love and power of God. Whatever hinders me I ought sensibly to discard. Whatever helps me I should embrace wholeheartedly. Entanglements hinder. Good food is vital to growth.

My commitment is something that ought to grow stronger and become a way of life as I continue to serve and obey the great God who is King of kings and Lord of all.

Belief is a matter of action. I need to trust God in a practical way, and submit my will to his. I must learn to obey God.

. . . IN GOD, THE FATHER ALMIGHTY, CREATOR OF HEAVEN AND EARTH

'Almighty' proclaims a God who is great, a God who reigns, a God in control—even though I may not always fully understand the way in which he works.

'Father' indicates someone who willingly accepts responsibility for the well-being of his children. He is pledged in his own heart to do all in his power for their welfare.

The perfect father is always willing to be involved—to listen, to guide, to protect and to make available all he has for the benefit of his family.

* * * * * * *

If such an Almighty God does exist, I ought to respect and fear him. A sense of awe—overwhelming wonder, respect, fear and reverence—is something I would do well to encourage in my own heart. God is not to be trifled with.

* * * * * * *

If God consciously created heaven and earth, then he must have had a purpose in doing so. If he made me too, then I must be here for a purpose. So life has a purpose! It need not be pointless and empty. But that purpose is rooted in God and can be found only in him. The highest aim of all must be to know God and enjoy him.

* * * * * * *

If the answers to life are to be found with God, then I ought to listen to him. Knowing him becomes the most important thing in life. Everything else, while not unimportant, is clearly secondary.

* * * * * * *

As I think of the greatness, the majesty—call it what you will—of God, I realize my insignificance before him and how deserving he is of my worship and praise. Anything which leads me to trust myself over and against him, or presume upon his goodness, is at best illogical, at worst suicidal.

* * * * * * *

When I say 'God created . . .' or 'God made . . .' I say that whatever biological or chemical processes resulted in the creation of the universe (and me!), these were begun and then controlled by the great Lord God.

I do not say I know in detail the exact means by which he achieved all this.

I do say that behind all life and creation is a personal and all-powerful force for good. That force is the living God. A loving, personal God created everything and everyone around me. We did not arrive simply as a result of a blind, impersonal process.

COSMIC CREATION COMPANY

MANUFACTURERS OF WORLDS ☆

Prop: GOD   Chief Engineer: GOD   Maintenance Engineer: GOD

Who created the universe and me is at least as important as *how* it happened. I would be wise to distinguish between these two questions. Much of the apparent conflict between modern science and my Christian faith would then disappear.

* * * * * * *

If I believe God created the universe and all life in it, then the most sensible thing I can do is live my life in harmony with his plan:

- for me—seeing myself as God sees me, seeing my life as God sees it;
- for others—valuing them as God values them, treating them as God treats them;
- for the world in which I live, respecting it as a gift from God to be enjoyed and developed, something to be co-operated with, not exploited or destroyed. As a people we should not pollute our environment or waste natural resources. We should be responsible caretakers of what God has given us.

God made heaven as well as earth. Right away I have to get used to the idea that there is a life beyond this one. This life is just meant to be a beginning.

* * * * * * *

It would be foolish to do anything in this short life which would damage my readiness for the life that is to come. Also, I will never really understand this life, and God's pattern of living for it, until I begin to view it with heaven in mind. God is wanting to get me ready!

A sense of awe is something I would do well to encourage in my own heart. God is not to be trifled with.

I BELIEVE IN JESUS CHRIST, HIS ONLY SON, OUR LORD

When I see Jesus Christ described as the *only* Son of God I realize immediately there is something very special about him, something unique which raises him far above the level of every other religious figure. We are left no room for compromise over the uniqueness of Christ. Either he is the *only* Son of God, our Lord, and thus above all others, or else he is nothing but the most shallow and deceitful of impostors.

* * * * * * *

If Jesus is unique and the *only* Son of God, just where does that leave all the other religions? Well, for a start, it does not mean that their followers are necessarily any less sincere in their beliefs than I am. It does mean, though, that the *full* truth of God is found only in Jesus—and only in Jesus is it guaranteed to be clear and uncorrupted. While other religions may contain various degrees of truth in their teaching, they offer at best only a shadow—and at worst a monstrous perversion—of the full, true glory of God.

However attractive and apparently tolerant, the idea that all religions lead to God is rubbish. They don't! They teach gods of vastly different natures. They teach different understandings of mankind and his role in this life and the next. They say very different things about what God wants to do in our lives, and what our response to this should be. And they also disagree on the very important question, 'How do I come to know God?'

" I find it far easier to think of God as JESUS than to imagine a distant BEING who does everything. "

During his life on earth, Jesus showed by his teaching and miracles the love God has for everyone. He also clearly showed how God could transform every area of our lives, and meet our every need, if only we would follow him. In a most challenging way he also showed what sort of people God wants us to be—people like him! When we see Jesus we see God. But also, when we see Jesus we see the way God wants *us* to be.

Jesus Christ claimed complete equality with God. He said he and God were one. It was because of this that the Jewish leaders had him crucified. Gradually, through the teaching of Jesus both before and after his resurrection, it became apparent to his followers that God, in some way beyond their complete understanding, had three equal aspects of his nature:

God the Father—who has always existed and who planned the creation of the universe and the rescue (salvation) of mankind from the consequences of their rebellion against himself (sin).

Jesus Christ—God the Son—who also has always existed and who at one time came from God the Father and lived among us as a man. In a manner beyond our complete grasp Jesus was both fully God and fully man. By his life and self-sacrifice on the cross Jesus proclaimed and secured God's way of salvation for all who would receive it from him. This salvation is his free gift of love. On the cross Jesus took upon himself physically and spiritually the full fury of God towards sin, so that we might be forgiven and receive a new life in his name. Extraordinary—but true!

The Holy Spirit—God the Holy Spirit—who is the agent through whom God has always worked in the world, the church and the individual. Since the victorious return of Jesus to heaven the Holy Spirit has been available to us all as individuals. His desire is to place within us the life of Christ and equip us with the full power of God himself for daily living.

The fact that Jesus is not just Lord but *our* Lord, *my* Lord, has deep implications for my life. It means I must live subject to his love, and to what he wants, at all times. It means every area of my life—my attitudes, ambitions, money . . . everything—must be laid at his feet and made available for him to direct as he knows best. If I am not obeying Jesus in a practical way, then there is no point in my calling him my Lord. I may fool other people that he is. I might even fool myself. But I will not fool him.

* * * * * * *

That Jesus is Lord means much more than that he is just someone whose position I acknowledge, or whose teaching I accept. It means that in practice my final responsibility in life is to him—not to my career, my home, my family, or to anything or anyone else but him.

This does not mean that I am opting out. As I open myself to Jesus he makes me *more*, not less, aware of my earthly duties in different spheres. He also gives me the incentive and encouragement to carry them out.

* * * * * * *

Jesus Christ is the foundation of my Christian faith. Without Christ there is no Christianity. I am not committed to a philosophy, a way of life, or to any particular church. I am committed to Christ. Obviously my commitment to him does involve certain beliefs, and a particular style of living, and loyalty to others in my church. However, these things are the consequences of my primary commitment to Jesus Christ, God himself, who loved me and gave his life for me.

What's more, since his resurrection this Jesus continues to live. He reigns over the universe and wants to reveal in my life the down-to-earth nature of his love and power in action.

"You say that you believe in the Divine Light Theosophy and the Ultimate Cosmic Principle? Actually I'm just a follower of Jesus."

If anyone ever asks me what my Christian faith is all about, the answer is Jesus, God's ultimate revelation of himself to man; Jesus, God himself, who lived and walked on this earth so that we might come to know him.

If anyone ever asks me what my Christian faith is all about, the answer is ... Jesus!

HE WAS CONCEIVED BY
THE POWER OF THE HOLY SPIRIT...

Right from the start I have to get used to the idea that there is a supernatural element to my belief in Jesus Christ. This is nothing for me to be embarrassed about or make excuses for. It is neither illogical nor unreasonable. It has nothing to do with ghosts or hobgoblins at the bottom of the garden. I am doing no more than saying that some of the ways of God are beyond my limited understanding. They are simply ways beyond the normal laws of nature by which God intervenes in his created world.

"Man! You surely can't expect me to believe in all that supernatural stuff about God!! Now, talk to me about U.F.O's, men from outer space and the paranormal, and I'm with you all the way."

Perhaps the most surprising thing about any supernatural workings of God is that I should be disturbed by them. I ought to be encouraged and comforted by them instead. If God is God then, by definition, some of his actions are going to be beyond my immediate understanding. If I *could* completely understand God I would have far more cause for concern. I would then have him 'worked out' and 'under control'. I would begin to see myself as being on a par with him. At that moment he would cease to be God Almighty and become just another contender for ultimate control of the universe.

*   *   *   *   *   *   *

A subtle form of pride often causes much of the difficulty I have in accepting the more extraordinary ways of God. When it comes to it I am just the same as Eve, in the garden of Eden, who was not prepared to trust God, but had to experience and 'know' everything for herself. My pride demands to know what God is perhaps not ready to reveal. Certainly it doesn't like the idea of anyone thinking me silly for believing in God. Often I am not prepared to wait for God to deal with a particular situation in his way and time. Sometimes my difficulties are the result of all of these things put together!

*   *   *   *   *   *   *

The fact that God wants me to trust him and accept that I will never fully understand all his ways in this life, does not mean he wants me dead from the neck up! Far from it! He wants my mind alert and active, eager to receive more and more truth about himself as he reveals it to me. It's just that, in the long run, he wants me to acknowledge that he has the right to reveal or not to reveal!

"And is there any cure for being 'dead from the neck up' doctor?"

As I go on trusting and following Christ I find the main reason for much of my ignorance of his ways is not his secretiveness, but my unwillingness to listen and give him the chance to explain. If I don't learn to sit quietly before the Lord, more intent on listening to him than telling him what I think he needs to hear, then it is totally unfair of me to accuse him of never telling me anything. He doesn't get the chance!

* * * * * * *

So I cannot fully understand how God could directly conceive a child through the action of his Spirit in the womb of a woman. That is beyond human comprehension. However, if God is almighty, then it is a perfectly possible thing for him to do.

The main reason for much of my ignorance of God's ways is not his secretiveness but my unwillingness to listen and give him the chance to explain.

. . . AND BORN OF THE VIRGIN MARY

The supernatural element in God's ways is demonstrated very clearly in the conception of Jesus by the Holy Spirit in his virgin mother's womb.

Yet the fact that God bothered to involve a human being at all in the coming of his Son shows equally that his interests are very much rooted among us here on earth. We have a God still passionately interested in every aspect of his creation. He longs that we, the crown of his creation, should know him not just in a vague or theoretical way, but intimately through his personal involvement in our lives. He genuinely wants us to share in the excitement of seeing him at work among us.

* * * * * * *

There is of course something very special about the Virgin Mary. She alone had the privilege of carrying the Son of God in her womb. God was able to use her in this way simply because she trusted him enough to act in accordance with his will. This is surely what led to God granting her the supreme honour of bearing his only Son.

On one occasion after Jesus' ministry had begun, a woman cried out, 'Blessed is the womb that bore you, and the breasts that you sucked!' Jesus replied, 'Blessed rather are those who hear the word of God and keep it!' Such faith and obedience were the prime virtues of Mary.

* * * * * * *

Every one of us can, like Mary, be caught up in a work of God and know his power in our lives. We too may know the reality of his presence and working—if we trust him, and are willing to obey him.

* * * * * * *

Jesus was born in the same way as you and I. If we had been there we could have witnessed the birth with our own eyes, and held him in our own arms. Jesus is an historical figure in the same way as Julius Caesar, Henry VIII, Winston Churchill and others. His knowledge of the life we lead is not just an academic one obtained by watching us from heaven. He has been through it all himself. He knows exactly what it feels like have to earn a living, cope with family difficulties and generally come to terms with life.

* * * * * * *

In every sense Jesus is the pioneer calling us to follow where he has already gone, rather than the general ordering his troops to advance while he

"That's it ... stout fellows! Remember I am always right there – behind you!"

remains safe in his comfortable quarters well away from the heat of the battle. Jesus is a visible demonstration of the fact that God is ready and waiting to involve himself with us on every level of our daily living.

* * * * * * *

God chose a humble peasant woman to give birth to his only Son, and didn't even wait until she was married before bringing on the signs of pregnancy in her body. If at any time I want to excuse my unavailability to the Lord by saying, 'I don't have the contacts, I'm not influential enough,' or, 'I don't have the money or the education,' then the chosen role of Mary offers me little comfort. God does not need 'important' people to achieve his purposes. He just needs people who are available.

" The trouble is when I tell the Lord I'm too young- inexperienced - untrained- unready - uncertain and really no use, I sometimes have to stop for breath- and I find he is still saying, 'It's you I want!'"

On the other hand, if I secretly pride myself on my wealth, my ability, or my social status, then I need to watch out. God may well give me a miss if, in my heart, I am looking down on other members of his family. If I see security in my social or financial position then it is false—and it is blindness. The only true security is in the faithfulness and power of the living God.

* * * * * * *

Unfortunately, God often does not spare our blushes! An embarrassed Joseph seriously thought about calling it all off when he found out that his fiancée was pregnant. We will not go far along the road with Christ before realising that, occasionally, there may be a clash between maintaining our respectability (in the worst sense of the word!) before man, and our obedience to God.

God loves all men, but he has a special commitment to the underprivileged in any community. The poor, the hungry, the helpless and the diseased won a special affection from Jesus during his time on earth. God feels for them and is committed to relieving their distress. Christ himself was born into a poor family.

* * * * * * *

Jesus came to improve the lot of all mankind and to awaken our sense of responsibility towards each other. He emphasized forcibly that we have a direct *personal* responsibility for helping the needy, both in our own community and in the world at large. He detests oppression, exploitation, prejudice or injustice of any kind. He has promised that one day he will expose and destroy all of these things.

"Hey, look at this:
'Wanted. Young
believers, no previous
experience necessary.
Willing to go anywhere,
do anything, any time
Applicants please pray?"

I may not have realized it, but I now have a share in God's commitment towards the needy. That commitment is to help relieve their suffering by whatever practical means I can. It will mean personal sacrifice and involvement in some way. Even so, it is a commitment from which there is no opting out. If I turn my back on them, I am turning my back on Christ.

God doesn't need 'important' people to achieve his purposes. He just needs people who are available.

HE SUFFERED
UNDER PONTIUS PILATE...

As Roman rulers went Pontius Pilate was probably no different from many. He just had the unfortunate distinction of being the person under whose political authority the Son of God suffered. If I had been alive at the time I could have witnessed the arrest, trial, flogging and crucifixion of Jesus Christ. It would have been as horrific to see as the arrest and torture of any innocent man. Jesus understands very well what it is like to be the victim of religious or political persecution.

Evidence exists dating Pilate's time of office in the Roman Empire. Such evidence is one of the means by which the facts of the life of Christ can be firmly grounded in history. Jesus is no myth.

" I'd stop worrying Pontius dear— few people will get named in the Apostles' Creed."

There is no denying the problem of reconciling the existence of a loving, all-powerful God with the hideous fact of suffering in this life. Much of our suffering is clearly the result of our own stupidity

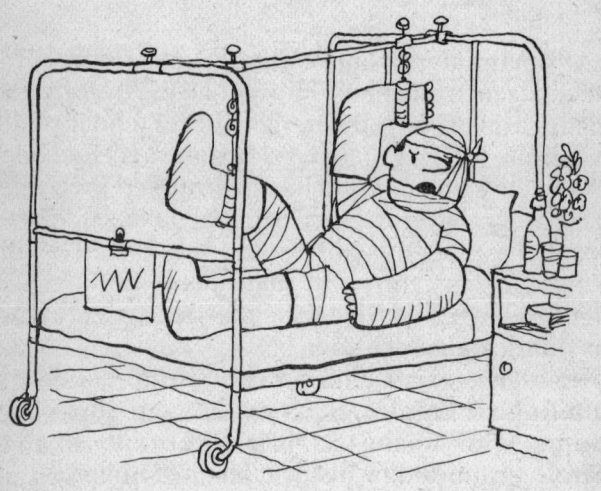

"Okay, I know it's all my own fault, but that's no comfort..."

and man's inhumanity to other men. But we still have to admit that we don't have all the answers to the apparently undeserved poverty, disease, hunger, mental illness and physical deformation which befall so many people in the world.

* * * * * * *

To say we do not know the answer to suffering does not mean there isn't one. Our understanding is limited. The Bible may give only a partial answer to the problem of why people suffer, but it does clearly indicate God's attitude to suffering. He hates it. Moreover, in Christ he is working to overcome it and one day eliminate it completely. Scripture treats the problem of suffering from a practical, not academic viewpoint.

* * * * * * *

The Bible regards suffering as an intrusion into God's created world. Creation was made good and free from pain. Suffering came in as a consequence of sin, man's rebellion against God. While Christ may give us the means to cope with suffering, and even bring good out of it, it will not be finally abolished until he returns to establish the new heaven and earth he promises.

* * * * * * *

Jesus was very realistic in his approach to suffering. He warned us not to build our hopes and happiness on this world. It is a sinful world and, therefore, suffering will always be present. Eventually we will lose all that there is of this world, so it is our eternal relationship with God that ultimately counts.

* * * * * * *

Suffering does not always have to be disastrous. If our response is basically one of submission and trust in the love of God it can produce character, understanding and a deeper awareness of Christ's love and power. Wrong reactions on our part merely pile the additional anguish of bitterness and resentment on top of any suffering already present.

* * * * * * *

Christ was suffering in my place. He was completely innocent. He had done nothing wrong to bring such torment upon himself. He was suffering on my behalf, taking upon himself the punishment that, by rights, should have been mine; punishment due as a consequence of the wrong I have done in my life. He did this because he loves me.

* * * * * * *

Christ's experience of suffering was intense and real. Jesus is described by Scripture as the 'Suffering Servant' and one who is 'acquainted with grief'. He died an agonizing death and went to lengths of extraordinary pain so that I might enjoy a relationship of love with him. I can gain real comfort from the living presence of this same Jesus in any suffering of my own.

* * * * * * *

Often I have a sadly narrow-minded understanding of suffering. To me it seems so much about physical pain and discomfort. However, I would do well to consider the spiritual grief Jesus must have endured simply living in this world for thirty years or so. Looking around and seeing greed, exploitation, disease and injustice eating away at his creation must have been heartbreaking —in many ways perhaps more painful than his eventual crucifixion.

In the garden of Gethsemane immediately before his arrest Jesus was not suffering physically at all, yet his spiritual awareness of the situation left him in agony. I ought to consider opening up my heart more to the Spirit of Jesus so that I might share these sufferings of his also. All too often things which grieve or anger Jesus leave me completely unmoved.

Suffering is an intrusion into God's creation. He hates it and, in Christ, he is working to overcome it and one day eliminate it completely.

. . . WAS CRUCIFIED, DIED, AND WAS BURIED

Even with the full range of modern technology at our disposal we have not yet come up with a more unpleasant way of killing one another than by crucifixion. It was both painful and prolonged. It was the Romans' ultimate deterrent.

* * * * * * *

Jesus suffered physically in a horrible way. He also endured a spiritual anguish perhaps worse than any physical agony. On the cross God allowed Jesus to experience the spiritual desolation that would have been ours had he not hung there in our place. *My God, my God, why have you forsaken me?* was the despairing cry of a man whose perfect life-long fellowship with God the Father had been shattered, and against whom every force of evil was being unleashed. The taunts of the soldiers and watching crowd merely added to his torment.

And the answer to the question *why?* . . . so that we might live.

* * * * * * *

Jesus was dead when taken down from the cross. There is no reasonable doubt about that.

"All for me?"

Theories that he had merely fainted or entered into a temporary coma of some description are far more fanciful than the facts of the matter. In addition to the terrible wounds inflicted by the crucifixion itself, a spear was put through Jesus' side to ensure his death. He was too controversial a figure for them to take any chances.

* * * * * * *

Jesus was crucified for me. He took upon himself the most humbling and torturous of deaths to avoid my having to die. He died for my sin. His life was not taken from him involuntarily. He chose to give it as an undeniable demonstration of his love for me.

* * * * * * *

Only Christ could have died for my sins and for the sins of the world, because only he was both man (yet sinless) and God. Because he was fully man he could be our representative and bear our sin. Because he was fully God his life was infinite in its value and, therefore, could be offered for the sins of all men for all time.

* * * * * * *

Christ's offering of himself on the cross fully satisfies both the total hostility of God towards sin (which is judged) and his inexhaustible love for the sinner (who is forgiven). At the cross God is pardoning our sin without selling short his holy justice. In Christ, he takes the full penalty for sin—death—upon himself.

Jesus hangs on the cross as the most powerful demonstration of love in action that the world has ever seen. His cross is the place of both the *judgement* of our sin (and all the suffering it has caused) and our *deliverance* from sin and judgement.

* * * * * * *

Through his completed work on the cross Jesus Christ has cleared the way for our rescue ('salvation') from the power and consequences of sin. But to make the work of Jesus real for me I have to respond. I need consciously to *accept* his offer of forgiveness. The new life he is offering becomes mine only when I admit my sin and turn from it, and receive Christ into my life as Saviour and Lord through a personal commitment to him.

* * * * * * *

So many different emotions must have been tearing the hearts of Jesus' family and friends as he was buried. So many dreams must have been shattered as the lifeless body was laid down and the tomb sealed. Yet, in fact, it was just the beginning. It will save me no end of trouble in my own Christian life if I start to understand now that the experience of the cross—death and resurrection—is at the heart of Christian living. I have to learn to trust.

Often God is only just beginning to work when humanly all seems lost. I have to be prepared to follow Christ in obedient faith to this position of 'death' and risk actual failure. If not, then I am never clearly going to know in my own experience his power to bring new life into situations that appear to be hopeless.

* * * * * * *

When I am 'dead'—and know it—then clearly, from that point on, God is my only hope. My own resources are spent. It is God or nothing!

This may sound a wonderfully spiritual position to be in. It can also be desperately nerve-racking! But it does work! Only if I trust Christ sufficiently to follow him to that point of 'death' will I ever discover this fully.

Jesus was crucified for me. He took upon himself the most humbling and painful death to avoid my having to die.

HE DESCENDED TO THE DEAD

This sentence of the Creed may also be translated, 'He descended into hell,' although for reasons stated below that is not a very helpful translation when talking of Christ's descent.

* * * * * * *

However embarrassing it may be, there is no escaping the fact that Christ taught that everybody passes on to an after-life either in heaven or hell. Life now may be compared to this future life in the same way as the life of an unborn child in its mother's womb may be compared to its life after birth. One day we will all know the truth of this.

* * * * * * *

Scripture indicates two areas of life beyond the one we are currently experiencing. There is heaven (where God is and evil isn't) and hell (where evil is and God isn't).

Several Greek and Hebrew words are translated by our word 'hell'. The Hebrew word *Sheol* and the Greek *Hades* refer to that realm of the dead into which God has thrown the fallen angels who

"God wouldn't send people to hell... would he?"

originally rebelled against him. The dead human wicked are confined there too. Here they await God's final judgement upon them at the end of time. It was to this place of the dead that Jesus descended after his death and proclaimed to the evil spirits there his victory on the cross.

The other word employed—*Gehenna*—indicates the final destiny and state of punishment of all who reject God. The Bible refers to this *Gehenna* hell with a disturbing clarity and regularity. It is under God's rule but a place from which he has chosen to withdraw his presence and working.

In short, hell is where God isn't. It is a horrible reality.

* * * * * * *

There are no easy answers as to how a loving God can send people to hell. However, if individuals have chosen to reject God and the life he offers them, then, apart from over-ruling their freely made decision, God can only allow them to have their own way. In that sense, God does not send anyone to hell—people choose to go.

A far more serious charge to level against a loving Creator would be that, knowing the perils ahead, he does nothing either to warn or rescue us from them. Given his respect for our freedom of choice, the most God can do is issue constant warnings of hell and provide a way out for those who want it—

Warnings have come throughout history through prophets, in Scripture, and through straight-forward preaching of God's word.

A way out has been provided, in love, through Christ's act of self-sacrifice on the cross.

If we choose to reject God's warning, then it is both unreasonable and absurd to blame him for the consequences. If we cut ourselves off from the author of life . . . we die.

Hell is where God isn't. It is a horrible reality . . . but one that no one need experience.

ON THE THIRD DAY HE ROSE AGAIN

The central fact at the heart of the Christian gospel is that Jesus Christ rose from the dead. The cross was the beginning, not the end, of Christianity. The simple early message that changed the lives of individuals and communities as it swept across the Roman empire was 'Jesus is risen'.

The Apostle Paul saw this fact as being so crucial to the belief of the first Christians that he wrote, 'If Christ has not been raised, then our preaching is useless, and so is your faith.'

"Okay men, you can fall out-the party's over, the stone's in place and that's the end of it..."

That a man should be raised from the dead is an extraordinary claim. But Jesus was more than just a man—he was also God. Many attempts have been made to provide other explanations for the events of the time. But actually, more faith is needed to believe them than the biblical record. The evidence of the empty tomb, the completely transformed lives of the disciples, and the various written accounts, are most reasonably explained by one fact—Jesus was risen!

* * * * * * *

The raising of Jesus from the dead at one moment in time is not just the most important event in the Christian faith. If it is true, it must be the most important event in history. No one else has been similarly resurrected! This single act alone puts Jesus into a totally different category from any other prophet, guru, wise man or leader. No one else has ever claimed such a resurrection for themselves.

* * * * * * *

The resurrection is the final confirmation that Jesus is God himself. It is also visible proof of his victory over death, and evidence of success in his mission to free us from that same power of sin and death. It is because Jesus lives that, by his Spirit, he is able to empower our lives and share with us the victory he has won.

Christians are people who enjoy this living, personal union with Jesus Christ. They have the Spirit of Jesus living within them.

The resurrection of Jesus is our guarantee that forgiveness and a right relationship with God may be enjoyed in Jesus' name. The eternal God raised Jesus by his mighty power. This resurrection is God the Father's seal of approval on the ministry of his only Son. It is our assurance of the future resurrection to everlasting life that he promises us too. We will simply be following Jesus.

* * * * * * *

Following Christ means that my old self must 'die' so that a Mark II version of me can be raised to new life.

Spiritually, I have been crucified with Jesus. Because of this, I need to be careful that *all* of my old self remains dead on the cross. Of course, the more obviously unpleasant habits of my past have no place in me now. My bad language, my immorality, my dishonest and violent ways quite clearly do not belong in the kingdom of God.

But many of my apparently 'normal' ambitions and thoughts may also need renewing. Such things as my attitude towards my possessions, money, and my opinions of other people all need renewing. My over-riding ambition should now be to know Christ better. My priorities in this new life must now match those of the King!

* * * * * * *

It is because Christ rose from the dead and is alive still that we can grow to know him in a deepening relationship, just as with any other living person. You cannot have a relationship with a dead man! Jesus, by his resurrection, has demonstrated himself to be a living, reigning, conquering Lord. That is good news! It is also the very key to life itself—the gateway to knowing the living God who created and sustains us and all life around us.

* * * * * * *

The historical, bodily resurrection of Jesus is the very guts of the gospel. Without it there is no gospel. With it nothing is impossible, for truly God is with us and working among us as powerfully as he has ever done.

The question now is, just how open am I to what he wants to do in my life?

'Jesus is risen' is the heart of the gospel. A Christian is someone who enjoys a living, personal relationship with the risen Jesus.

HE ASCENDED INTO HEAVEN . . .

Some forty days after his resurrection Jesus removed his bodily presence from this earth and returned to his original relationship with God the Father. It was the final seal on the victory he had won. It was his triumphant return to his Father in heaven—mission accomplished! His final destination was not a cross. It was—and still is—a throne.

* * * * * * *

The return of Jesus to heaven was God's declaration—both to this world and to the invisible spiritual world—of Christ's total triumph over sin and death.

Moreover, his ascension marked a major development of his work here on earth. Far from ending all those years ago his ministry continues through the lives of those in whom his Spirit dwells. That work will continue without interruption until the day of his return.

* * * * * * *

Once Christ had ascended into heaven he was no longer limited in his working by the physical restriction of being in just one place at a time.

"We may have thought we got rid of him, but I get the feeling that he's still very much around."

Before ascending he promised the gift of his Spirit to all who believed in him and received him. After his return to heaven the Spirit was poured out, starting with the believers in Jerusalem. From that time onwards the work of Jesus could be reproduced wherever there was someone full of his Spirit.

* * * * * * *

Anything suggesting that by his ascension Jesus has 'gone away' or become remote is quite wrong. The disciples were worried about this very idea, so Jesus warned them of his coming arrest and crucifixion. To make the position quite clear, Jesus assured them, 'If anyone loves me he will obey my teaching. My Father will love him and we will come to him and make our home with him . . . Remain in me and I will remain in you.' Jesus is with us—actually *in* us—by his Spirit. Through the gift of the Holy Spirit, his involvement in our lives has been made personal and multiplied many millions of times over since his resurrection.

If I have opened my life to be filled and led by the Spirit of Jesus then I can expect things to happen. He will be making me more and more like himself, sharing with me his understanding and compassion.

I may also expect the full *power* of Jesus to be available to me. The Holy Spirit is very practical. I just have to learn consciously to depend on him for guidance and strength.

The final destination of Jesus was not a cross. It was—and still is—a throne.

. . . AND IS SEATED AT
THE RIGHT HAND OF THE FATHER

Something seems continually to be squeezing my mind into believing that God doesn't reign. It says, 'He's not fully in control; he can't be; look at the state of the world!' That same thing goes on to suggest the most terrible disasters may befall me if I apply Christ's teaching too exactly to key areas of my life, such as my family, career or possessions.

All of this is rubbish. God is in control. He always has been and always will be.

* * * * * * *

The fact that God does reign is occasionally going to annoy me. From time to time I like to resume control of my own interests. Usually this occurs when I am feeling fed up with one thing or another. I like to devise a way out of the situation.

Or else it may be that some driving force deep within me is not being satisfied in the way it demands. I want something. I may then try to create a situation which I believe will bring me fulfilment.

In fact, acting in this way and hiding from the true issues at these times is stupid. God won't be frightened by my tantrums! I will only pile up trouble for myself. The sensible answer is to put myself before the Lord in an attitude of submission and ask him to make his will my will too.

* * * * * * *

Kicking against God's way of working is not very smart—*he reigns!* It's like being a child who throws a temper when daddy won't give him any sweets. Learning to let go of such demands will be one of the most exhilarating experiences of my life. I will then begin to experience a deep freedom as these petty urges and areas of self-interest loosen their hold on me.

* * * * * * *

From his position of authority in heaven Jesus sees everything that happens on earth. Nothing escapes him. He is in control and directing his

forces to what he knows to be the best effect. Governments good and bad, multi-national companies, banks, powerful trade unions and political parties may appear to control what happens in the world. But they don't: God does.

Amazingly God wants to lift me alongside him so that I may understand more fully the world in which I live, and see the way he is working in it. I will then be able to live confidently and effectively as a Christian—as Jesus intended!

But for this to happen I must give Jesus my time. I must wait on him, look to him, listen to him, and absorb the teaching of God in Scripture.

* * * * * * *

Jesus sitting at the right hand of God is yet another source of assurance to me. He promised he would continually be speaking to God the Father on my behalf. Jesus is safeguarding my relationship with God the Father. Through him we always have access to God. We will never be turned away.

To know that Jesus is pitching in for me, particularly when I don't have the strength to fight for myself as I would like, just leaves me grateful and relieved. It is yet another of Christ's gifts of which I am totally undeserving. And any sweetness I may taste now in my relationship with him is but a mere foretaste of what is to come.

* * * * * * *

Jesus will ensure I receive all I need to live victoriously in this life. Whatever I require has

"O Lord - I can keep the first four rules and try for the last two - but the other four are just not on!"

already been given; it is there for me to draw on if only I will realize it. Jesus has the power and authority to act in my interests. My task is simply to make sure I remain obedient and open enough to receive what he is wanting to give.

Something continually seems to be squeezing my mind into believing that God doesn't reign... That is rubbish!

HE WILL COME AGAIN TO JUDGE THE LIVING AND THE DEAD

One day Jesus is going to return in a visible and undeniable way. The New Testament refers to this fact over 300 times. When he returns the dead will be raised and, along with those living at the time, their lives will be finally judged.

In many ways it is an unsettling thought that my life will be exposed before a holy and righteous God. Even more disturbing is the fact that many people will be banished from his presence because they have rejected him in this life. God will respect their decision, and the awful consequences of their choice will now be seen.

"It wasn't so much that I CHOSE....rather that I drifted."

If I feel I can get away with a bit of rebellion here and there, this uncompromising element in the teaching of Jesus will bring me up short.

* * * * * * *

When I'm in my right mind I can look forward to Jesus coming to judge the living and the dead with joy. I have no need to fear. On the cross, Jesus was offering to take upon himself all my hang-ups and prejudices, my jealousies, my resentments—my sin!—and to clear my cupboard of all its skeletons. I can take up his offer now and face him with confidence, happy that he knows me already and that my slate is clean in his name.

"How long have you been in there?"

In many ways it is more convenient to believe in total destruction or reincarnation after death than to accept the teaching of Jesus. He was quite clear, that after death comes judgement. That is morally demanding. It tells me there are standards of right and wrong in life which apply to everyone. It also implies strongly that it is possible for someone to fail to come up to those standards.

* * * * * * *

The prospect of a coming judgement does sometimes disturb me a lot. There are a number of aspects of my life of which I am not particularly proud. On most occasions I would rather just sweep them under the table and make out they weren't there. That won't work, though. There's no point in my trying to deceive Christ, particularly when he wants only to free me of these problem areas.

* * * * * * *

Keeping a clean sheet with God and the people around me is a sound principle on which to base my life. Unfortunately, I have the ability to foul things up with monotonous regularity. I very much need the continual cleansing Jesus offers when I honestly confess my failings in thought, word and deed. If I don't take advantage of this cleansing, then gradually my whole way of life becomes more and more polluted, until major repair work is necessary.

Getting into the habit of keeping clean, and making cleanliness in God's sight a priority, completely eliminates any fear of judgement. I

"I live by my own
standards, and
I'll die by them...."

need have nothing to hide. But that is not all: being clean is one of the most liberating experiences I can know.

* * * * * * *

The other joyful element in the return of Jesus is the confident knowledge that, by his judgement, one day justice shall rule the earth. When Jesus returns he will visibly overcome all the forces of greed and exploitation that appear to be in control in the world. Their time is limited; they do not reign. Our God reigns! One day the meek shall inherit the earth, and this world shall be cleansed of every evil power. This is not some imaginary hope but a sure promise from the mouth of Christ our risen, reigning, returning Lord.

Judgement is morally demanding. But getting into the habit of keeping clean in God's sight completely eliminates any fear it may hold for me.

I BELIEVE IN THE HOLY SPIRIT . . .

The Holy Spirit is God himself. He is a person. He is the agent through whom God works in the world, the church and the individual. Whatever God does he does through a work of his Holy Spirit.

* * * * * * *

God controls the universe by his Spirit. The same Holy Spirit perfectly dwelt in Jesus. He is now the driving force of the church supplying us with God's divine energy. It is the Holy Spirit who awakens our conscience to receive Christ and who is now his representative within us transforming our character into the likeness of Jesus.

In short, there is no Christian life outside of the Holy Spirit.

* * * * * * *

The Holy Spirit is God's gift of love to all who will receive him. The main issue for me is not so much whether or not I believe in the Holy Spirit, but have I opened my life to him? Do I allow him to have his way with me in the many different situations in my life?

" I thought I would leave asking for the Holy Spirit until I had been a Christian for a year or two... "

God wants to fill me with his Spirit. I have been greatly misled if I see being filled with the Spirit as an optional extra in my Christian life. It is for all who follow Christ. The Spirit is not reserved for any particular denomination or for any special types of Christian people. He is the very source of power, character and wisdom Jesus promised to all who would follow him. I must learn consciously to depend upon him in every area of my daily living. I need all his resources!

* * * * * * *

How am I filled with the Spirit? By asking. Jesus said, 'If a man is thirsty, let him *come* to me and *drink*. Whoever *believes* in me, as the Scripture has said, streams of living water *will flow* from within him.' Scripture records that 'he meant the Spirit, whom those who believed in him were later to receive'.

Am I thirsty? If so, I need only come to Christ, drink, believe, and the Spirit will flow, not because of how I may or may not feel, but because Jesus has promised. My only response is to say 'Thank you' and follow his leading.

As much as anything, Jesus wants to reproduce the characteristics of his life in my body. His love, his power, his purity, his sense of justice and righteousness, are all things he would love to bring out in my own being. But for this to happen it's no good simply trying hard to be a good boy (or girl)! I must realize that the most important thing in my life is to submit to the will of God. All the time I am submitted to him, and open to whatever his Spirit wishes to do with me or say to me, then Jesus has a clear path. My part is simply to obey.

* * * * * * *

The characteristics of Jesus which will appear in my life as a result of my obedience are known as 'the fruit of the Spirit'. They are one evidence of the reality of Jesus in a person's life.

The fruit of the Spirit is love, joy, peace, patience, kindness, goodness, faithfulness, gentleness and self-control. All these should be increasingly reflected in the life of anyone who has the Holy Spirit living within him. Just as an apple tree produces apples, and a plum tree produces plums, so the Holy Spirit produces his fruit wherever he makes his home. We should all bear fruit!

* * * * * * *

Besides reproducing the characteristics of Jesus in my life, the Holy Spirit also wishes to give me the power to be an effective witness for him. God is a mighty God, a God committed to the establishing of his kingdom here on earth. He loathes suffering and disease, and is totally repulsed by injustice or evil of any kind. Jesus brought healing and new life wherever he went. God wants me to be an agent of his love in a similar way.

* * * * * * *

Gifts of the Spirit, like the very implanting of Jesus' life in our own, are another part of God's work which we call supernatural—that is, beyond our full understanding. They are weapons of love. They are the power of God which enables us to pray effectively, understand situations and, if necessary, intervene effectively in them. As we act with power in Jesus' name, so people will see his love in action. Things will happen!

* * * * * * *

How do I exercise spiritual gifts? By stepping out in faith, praying, and acting in the way I believe Jesus is leading me. As I step out, so God will respond by releasing through me the gift appropriate to my situation. The purpose of spiritual gifts is that God's love and power might be released through me for the benefit of *other people*.

I'll find it very hard to exercise gifts by just sitting down and examining my faith or my feelings, trying to find what gifts lie inside! Gifts are released by action, not by self-examination! They are present in the Spirit-filled believer by God's promise, not according to how I feel.

* * * * * * *

Gifts of the Spirit equip us for service. Rather than wasting time trying to rank them, we should use them sensitively in the context of serving God and loving our neighbour. Spiritual gifts are practical; they are given so that we may join in Christ's ministry and enjoy the same effectiveness that he had. They are not provided to satisfy any selfish motives or pride of our own. The credit for a gift belongs to the giver—Jesus! The prime role of the Holy Spirit is to bring glory and honour to Jesus.

* * * * * * *

The Holy Spirit is holy! That may sound obvious but, unfortunately, I tend to quickly forget its implications for my life. The Holy Spirit, by his very nature, cannot co-exist with sin. He is absolutely pure, separate and set aside for the work of representing Christ and extending God's kingdom here on earth. He is God himself and he lives in me! My unimpressive frame carries around a treasure beyond value—the Spirit of the living God. Only by staying clean, by confessing and turning away from any known sin in my life, can I maintain a clear relationship with God. Free from obstruction, his Spirit can then deepen his work of change within me. But if I hold on to what I know is wrong, then the Holy Spirit will quietly leave more and more areas of my life.

The Holy Spirit wants me clean! I need to remember that and watch what I get up to if I want him to stay.

The main issue is not so much whether I believe in the Holy Spirit...but have I opened my life up to him?

... THE HOLY CATHOLIC CHURCH ...

Jesus did not establish any denominations. His mission was to break the strangle-hold evil had upon his creation. He came to establish the truth about God and himself, and then see that truth put into practice in peoples' lives.

Jesus' concern was not with the exact form of service people attended. He came to establish the new Israel, the people of God, the fellowship of the Spirit. 'I will build *my* church,' he said! The church is the family of all those who love and obey Christ. It is his body here on earth. 'Catholic' means universal—that is, it includes *all* those who belong to Christ.

"I've never been able to say that bit about the 'holy Catholic church' because I was told I was a Protestant"

The church is much bigger than any denomination. It is the whole body of believers, worldwide, who accept Christ as their Saviour and honour him as Lord of their lives. The church is a holy people, not 'sacred' buildings. Bricks and mortar constitute nothing more than a convenient meeting place for believers.

"All my life I've worked hard to keep the church looking nice - and now you tell me it's not really the church at all!"

The church is a body which spans ages as well as continents; it includes those who have gone ahead of us in Christ and those who will follow. It is no small army!

* * * * * * *

The main problem with the church is that it is composed of thousands of people just like me! Everyone else is imperfect too! So the best thing I can do for the church, instead of criticizing it, is to let God work on my own imperfections! While he is doing that, my role is to help my fellow learners; I should be more concerned to encourage their good points than to condemn their bad ones.

*   *   *   *   *   *   *

The church—which includes me—is holy. That means 'set apart', like Jesus, distinctive in our life-style and priorities. It means that those things which I know are offensive to God have no part in my life. It means that my values and opinions come from him and nowhere or no one else. It means staying clean in God's eyes is very important to me.

*   *   *   *   *   *   *

The church has three clear priorities:

- we are to worship God sincerely, freely and enjoyably;

- we are able to live a life characterized by unity and genuine friendship as we allow the Holy Spirit to draw us together as one people under the lordship of Christ, regardless of age, race, wealth or social status;

- we are to witness to the truth of Jesus, his life, his death and resurrection for us, and the reality of his presence in our daily lives. We are to continue this ministry of proclaiming the good news!

When I become part of a whole body living for Christ in this way, then people will actually see that God is more than words and hot air. He is someone who can bring a new dimension to our life together

in this world. We will have an alternative society which, in the power of the Holy Spirit, *crosses* boundaries of race and social class rather than reinforcing them. This in itself will be an evidence of the living Jesus in our midst.

On the other hand, if we fail to become a community with our own identity, we will in effect be denying Christ. We will reduce his teaching to the level of a moral code—one among many—while we ourselves will be just another section of society going on in our own sweet way.

* * * * * * *

The church is a pilgrim people constantly moving on as we follow Christ. We should not be concerned about keeping things the way they are; we must continually step out after the Lord in our life together. It is as we step out that we will see God honouring our faith, clearly answering our prayers and supplying our needs.

This work of the Holy Spirit is essential. If we

don't move, then there are no needs for him to
provide for, or prayers to be answered! Above all
else it is the visible provision of God through
answered prayer which distinguishes the Christian
life from any other. We can't get by without
miracles!

*   *   *   *   *   *   *

People may not respond to it, but they cannot
deny a visible demonstration that God works!
Whether or not they benefit is up to the church—
and that means me and all the others like me who
go to make up 'the church'. If we feel that promoting
God's kingdom is important, then we'll live as he
wants. If we don't then we won't! It's as simple as
that. The decision is a perfectly straightforward
one, and the decision is ours.

---

*The church is not buildings. The church is a pilgrim
people constantly moving on as we follow Christ.*

"When I grow up I want
to be a Saint –
sing hymns, play a
harp and not
have to work ... "

Although it may take some getting used to, as a follower of Christ I am a member of his family here on earth. Despite my suspicions, none of the other members of the family are any less important in his eyes than I am.

* * * * * * *

Christ did not bring me into his family for me to live my life cut off from it. I will never begin to understand the richness of life in Jesus until I allow myself to be drawn into his body.

Establishing a separate body of my own—a new church—is not the ideal answer. It will just add yet another layer to the popular image of divided Christianity. And although at present I sincerely reject the possibility, it won't take so very long before my newly established group will become just as lifeless as many of the bodies I now reject.

Unfortunately, if I do want to split away, history is not on my side. The Bible shows God does not work through amputation. He restores from within rather than by promoting numerous splinter groups of Christian protesters.

* * * * * * *

Being part of God's family here on earth involves much more than just acknowledging its existence. It involves opening myself to its members and being willing to share my life with them, offering them encouragement, and being humble enough to draw strength from their support when I need it.

* * * * * * *

I might find it frightening at times, but entering into an open, honest relationship with people is a most liberating experience. Sharing with them what I am, as well as what I own, can have nothing less than a revolutionary effect on my life. It is all part of the distinctive life-style to which Christ calls us. If we are all living subject to the same Lord, and being dealt with by him according to the same principles, then we have so much we can teach and share with each other.

The whole notion of 'communion' runs far deeper than simply being a mutual admiration society, or some form of club. It is something active that looks out beyond itself rather than inwards. It means sharing a way of life. It means a community to which I must make my own contribution.

The overriding objectives of the Christian community are: growing to know Christ better in our own lives; and sharing his love with those around us, both believers and unbelievers.

* * * * * * *

Shortly before his arrest Christ told his followers to participate regularly in what has come to be known as Holy Communion, or the Eucharist. It involves the eating of bread and drinking of wine, as symbols of the body and blood of Christ which were given for us on the cross. It is an act of worship, remembrance and renewal, which is at the very heart of Christian life.

Feeding off the Lord, receiving forgiveness and being given a fresh start is the very essence of Christian living. It is at the Lord's table that I can quieten my heart and remember afresh the sacrifice of his life for me. Holy communion presents me with the formal opportunity to worship God and commit myself to him more faithfully in the coming days.

* * * * * * *

In the eyes of Jesus I am a saint. That doesn't mean I am any special breed of spiritual whizz kid, but just someone whose sins have been forgiven

"I never wanted to be a Saint, as I thought you had to be DEAD to qualify!"

and who acknowledges Christ as Lord of his life. God has a high impression of my potential in him. I'll do well to remember that, when my head drops at times.

* * * * * * *

The 'communion of saints' is much greater than just that visible fellowship of which I am part and parcel in this life. It is the total union in Christ of the *church militant*—those of us alive now on earth and engaged in the battle against evil—and the *church triumphant*—those who have physically died and are now in the presence of Jesus, living and reigning, waiting for me to join them.

'Communion' involves commitment…sharing… and contributing. It is something living and active. It means giving myself.

Essentially, *sin* is me deciding that I will play the role of God in my life. It is me pushing God out of his rightful place of authority and control. It is rebellion.

Sin always begins in my heart. What I may do or say later is just the consequence of what has already been allowed to take root in my heart.

"I could manage things better if I didn't find sin so attractive."

Sin is an affront to a holy God. It is also suicidal. God is completely committed to the destruction and elimination of all sin from his creation. People who line up against the Almighty God lose! If I choose to stand alongside what I know to be wrong then I am standing against God. In such a position my prospects are not exactly bright. . . .

* * * * * * *

The punishment for sin is death, separation from God who is the source of life. My sin would have led to death if Christ had not gone to the cross on my behalf. My forgiveness and life were won at great expense. God in no way turned a blind eye towards my sin, or imposed a lesser sentence on it; but the sinless Jesus was standing in my place.

* * * * * * *

Sin is like a disease. Like cancer it spreads, it rots and it eventually destroys both individual lives and whole communities. But it also has the habit of apprearing very attractive from time to time. I need to remember when I'm being lured, provoked, or otherwise tempted, that death is just round the corner.

* * * * * * *

I am a sinner! In thought, word and deed I have failed God, rebelled against him, disobeyed his commandments, wronged other people and completely cut myself off from him. I may not like to hear this if I consider myself a respectable member of the community. However, in God's eyes it is true. Whether I am a lord or lady of the realm, a guy or girl from the backstreets—or anywhere in between the two!—I am a sinner.

"Wow! That was a powerful sermon against sinners, Vicar. I just pray that everyone else took it to heart."

The good news of the gospel is that through Jesus Christ the hostility (caused by our sin) between ourselves and God has been removed. Our sins have been forgiven. Jesus has died in our place. God has accepted Jesus' sacrifice of himself on our behalf.

Jesus alone could have achieved this, because he was the only man who was perfect in every way. Anyone less than perfection could not have been acceptable as our representative in God's sight. It was because he had no sin of his own to account for that he was able to take our sin upon himself. In Jesus God is offering us the gift of forgiveness and new life.

* * * * * * *

As with any gift, I only benefit from it when I actually accept what I am being offered. Looking at a gift, admiring it, or even reading about it, does not make it mine. So I must consciously accept Jesus' gifts of forgiveness and a new life if I wish to experience them in reality.

* * * * * * *

Having once escaped the furious anger of God that was, by rights, coming my way, I will do well to look after myself more carefully in the future and keep clear of sin.

Unfortunately, I have this habit of acting rather like a man who, once rescued from the raging sea, insists on jumping straight back in again to get on with the business of drowning! By any standards this is lunacy!

* * * * * * *

I need to treasure my forgiveness and not presume upon it. It is nothing less than the gift of life itself. I can never be too thankful to Christ for his gift to me. Genuine thankfulness often does not come easily to me. Making empty noises of gratitude presents no problems (I can practise them!) but sadly, thanking Jesus from the heart often does.

I would be wise to ask God so to work on my heart of stone that he softens it into something which can feel and express genuine gratitude freely and openly. Such praise will be music to his ears and an invaluable foundation upon which to base my life in Christ.

I need to treasure my forgiveness and not presume upon it. It is nothing less than the gift of life itself.

. . . THE RESURRECTION
OF THE BODY . . .

I am never going to die in the sense of all my lights
going out and not coming back on again. If I am a
Christian I am going to pass from my present state
of living to a different state, but one which will be
perfection, not total destruction or any sort of
reincarnation. Part of that change will involve my
being given a new body.

"Lord! Not necessarily
a Miss World body,
but something a little
better than the one
I've got."

As yet I don't know exactly what this new body will be like—and neither does anyone else, except Christ. I do know it will not be subject to the physical limitations and aging that afflict my present frame. This different body will be the perfectly designed vehicle for my life in heaven, and will be free from all the ravages of sin with which I have to struggle in this life.

"What do you mean 'Going to church is not enough'?"

Everyone gets resurrected whether they believe it now or not. That's not entirely good news, because after death comes judgement. Many will have chosen eternal death by the way they have lived their lives and by their attitude to Christ. This is a horrible thought. It is also a very unpopular one today, when we all prefer to think we can get away with whatever we like and 'do our own thing'. This is not true. We are responsible to God. Whatever we may choose to believe at present, one day we will all find ourselves standing before Christ and having to give account of our lives.

* * * * * * *

Obviously, my new body will not be just a rehash of the old one. At the end of this life the physical body ceases to function and disintegrates. Any undertaker knows that! My new heavenly body will be a fresh, perfectly designed vehicle totally appropriate for my new home.

"Zero! Just wait till I tell my husband about that!"

Writing of the difference between our present physical bodies and our new heavenly bodies, the apostle Paul said, 'The body that is sown is perishable, it is raised imperishable; it is sown in dishonour, it is raised in glory; it is sown in weakness, it is raised in power; it is sown a natural body, it is raised a spiritual body.'

* * * * * * *

After his own resurrection Jesus had a noticeably different body. He travelled considerable distances by unknown means; he appeared in rooms from nowhere; he was often not immediately recognized; he was not subject to disease or decay. However, he was most clearly not a ghost, for he was real and recognizable when he spoke or did something familiar to his companions. He was apparently identified by the personality that his body conveyed.

My resurrection body will convey me in a similar way when, at death, my personality is released from the restrictions of this life. It will be the perfect means to convey the new me in my proper home—heaven!

Everyone gets resurrected. Whether we believe it now or not, one day we will all find ourselves standing before Christ, having to give account of our lives.

"Stupid really—
I keep looking
at my watch."

At present I cannot fully understand the idea of everlasting life. If I'm honest, at times the prospect hasn't exactly excited me. I saw it merely as an extension of this life minus the difficulties and plus some gooey sort of happiness. The thought of having to endure that for ever was daunting. However, I was wrong—heaven is nothing like that.

Heaven is a place of perfection. It is where God is and evil isn't. It is not somewhere inhabited solely by lovers of hymns and the harp, but a place in which life, in every sense of the word, is lived to the full as God originally intended. It is unbroken fellowship with Christ and a full appreciation of all that God is, all he has done, all he has given us.

While at present I may not completely see how that works out in detail, it is still a very exciting prospect indeed.

* * * * * * *

Life beyond death is an essential part of my belief in Christ. There is much more to come than what is in this life. Moreover, until I start looking at this life from a heavenly point of view, I'll never get anywhere near a full understanding of much of Jesus' teaching. He teaches with eternity in mind, as well as this life. Eternity is where I belong. Jesus is trying to get me ready for it. I am part of this life for just a short while. My values and priorities here and now should most naturally be those of heaven.

* * * * * * *

The certainty of life after death is a vital part of my Christian faith. If I am not careful my confidence in this may be watered down in an attempt to make my beliefs appear more reasonable to unbelieving friends. If this happens I will in fact lose much of the essence of Christian faith. Very quickly I will end up believing little more than they probably do.

" Of course I realize that the next ten minutes are not much in terms of eternity, but I do happen to be very hungry."

There is nothing unreasonable about the idea of life after death. Thousands of people demonstrate daily their fascination with the possibility of a life beyond this one. They turn out in crowds to watch different varieties of occult films or psychic cabaret acts. They purchase increasing numbers of books on occult subjects. The fact is that Jesus alone has the true answer to this question—and he actually came back from the dead to prove his point!

As in all other areas of my life, as a follower of Christ I need to have genuine confidence in him, and believe that everything he says is true. As it happens, it is!

Life beyond death is an essential part of my belief in Christ. There is much more of what is to come than there is of this life.

AMEN

Amen is a translation of an old Hebrew word. Essentially it means, 'So be it.' When I say it I say that I will accept what God does in answer to prayer, and I acknowledge that his way is best. I now submit myself to the will of God in the matter.

That's the problem! I'm very good at saying, 'Thy will be done,' and fairly competent at appearing to accept whatever that brings. But very often in my heart I am a long way from being happy, submitted or satisfied. *Amen* is much more than a spiritual full-stop at the end of a prayer. It implies an act of submission.

"Let's modernize the word and say, 'It's okay by me Lord, I'm with you all the way - over to you Lord'"

Submitting to Christ is very easy . . . when it involves agreeing to what I would probably have done anyway, or when it only affects something relatively unimportant to me. If I keep my submission just at this superficial level, I will never know the reality of Jesus in anything like the way he intends. That will be my fault, not his. I will start to find out how committed or submitted I am only when Jesus makes a claim on something precious to me—or else leads me in a direction I would not have chosen for myself.

If I genuinely trust him I will follow and obey him at these times, even though it may involve quite a battle within me. If I don't trust him, then I will go my own way or try to compromise.

*　*　*　*　*　*　*

As I begin to understand its full meaning, *Amen* can become a real source of peace in my life. It can mean that I've laid an issue before my Lord, opened myself to him, and ended up by saying, 'But the important thing is that you do what you know is best.'

From that point on I need have no worries. I may safely stand aside from the internal stresses and strains which plague the life of so many people. I am not opting out. I am saying quite simply, 'I have handed over my case to the King. I am bowing before a superior authority who, mercifully, happens to love me and have my best interests at heart.'

*　*　*　*　*　*　*

Using *Amen* as an act of submission is saying, 'I believe in God and in Jesus Christ, and that belief is something. which works itself out in a down-to-earth way in my everyday life. It makes a difference to the way I live, and to what sort of person I am.' If my belief in Jesus Christ does not do this then, in all honesty, it is of little relevance either to myself or to the world in which I live.

Amen is not just a spiritual full-stop at the end of a prayer. It implies an act of submission. If my commitment to Jesus Christ does not work itself out in this practical way, then it is of little relevance to me or to anyone else.

BIBLE REFERENCES

I believe
Psalms 99:1–5; 96:10–13; Luke 11:1–4; Ezekiel 33:11–16; Psalms 90:2; 93:2; Hebrews 11; James 2:14–26; John 14:13–14; Philippians 4:4–7; Philippians 3:13–14.

In God, the Father almighty, creator of heaven and earth
Hosea 11:1–4; Psalm 139:1–18; Exodus 3:1–6; Psalm 27:4; John 17:3; Genesis 1–2; Psalms 8, 104; 2 Corinthians 3:18.

I believe in Jesus Christ, his only Son, our Lord
John 14:6; Acts 4:12; John 10:30; 14:5–12; Colossians 1:15–20; 2 Corinthians 13:14; Philippians 2:5–11; John 14:23; Romans 10:8–9.

He was conceived by the power of the Holy Spirit
Isaiah 55:8–9; Proverbs 9:10; Luke 1:26–35; Isaiah 45:9–12; Romans 12:1–2; Proverbs 8:34.

And born of the Virgin Mary
Matthew 1:18–21; Isaiah 6:8; Acts 4:18–20; Hebrews 4:15–16; 12:1–2; Jeremiah 9:23–24; Matthew 25:31–45; James 2:14–24.

He suffered under Pontius Pilate
Luke 22:39–23:25; Isaiah 53:1–6, Hebrews 2:18, 1 Peter 2:22–25, Genesis 1–3, Isaiah 65:17–25.

Was crucified, died, and was buried
Mark 15:21–47; Matthew 16:21–24; 1 Peter 3:18; Mark 8:34–35; Romans 5:8; John 11:25–26; 2 Corinthians 5:17; Romans 12:1–2.

He descended to the dead
Matthew 10:28; 13:40–42, 47–50; 1 Peter 3:18–20; 2 Thessalonians 1:8–10; John 3:16–17.

On the third day he rose again
Luke 24; John 20; Acts 4:8–12; 10:38–41; Galatians 5:24; 1 John 4:4; Romans 6:3–7; 2 Corinthians 5:17; Romans 12:2; 1 Corinthians 15:1–8, 14.

He ascended into heaven
Hebrews 1:1–4; John 14:1–3; Acts 1:6–14; 2:1–4; 1 Timothy 3:16; Ephesians 1:20–21; Hebrews 9:24; John 14:12–14.

And is seated at the right hand of the Father
Romans 8:31–34; Job 40:1–5; Ephesians 1:16–21; 2:6–10; Hebrews 7:24–25; Romans 5:1–5.

He will come again to judge the living and the dead
Matthew 24–25; Luke 17:20–37; Acts 1:11; 17:31; Revelation 1:7; Hebrews 3:18; 1 John 1:9; Colossians 3:1–17; 2 Corinthians 5:10; 2 Peter 3:3–10.

I believe in the Holy Spirit
Genesis 1:1–4; Zechariah 4:6; John 14:15–17; 16:7–15; Romans 8:9–14; Ephesians 5:18; Galatians 5:13–26; Acts 1:8; 2:1–4; 4:31; 19:1–3; 1 Corinthians 12–14; Acts 3:1–10; 1 Corinthians 6:19–20.

The holy catholic church
Colossians 1:18; Ephesians 1:22–23; 2:19–22;
4:11–16; John 4:23–24; 1 Corinthians 12:12–31; 1
Peter 2:1–10; Psalm 149:1–5; Ephesians 3:8–12;
Matthew 28:16–20; Hebrews 2:1–4.

The communion of saints
Acts 4:32–37; James 2:1–9; 5:13–16; Hebrews
10:24–25; Ephesians 4:11–16; Romans 12:3–11;
Mark 14:17–25; 1 Corinthians 11:23–26; 1 John
5:4.

The forgiveness of sins
Isaiah 59:12–13; Psalm 14:1–3; Romans 3:23; Mark
7:17–23; Romans 6:23; 5:6–8; 1 Peter 2:24; Nahum
1:1–3; Galatians 5:1; 1 John 1:8–9; 1 Peter 1:14–19;
Psalm 139.

The resurrection of the body
John 5:28–29; 11:25; 1 Corinthians 15:35–58;
Hebrews 9:27; Romans 14:10–12; Revelation
20:11–12; 1 Thessalonians 4:14–17; 2 Thessalonians 1:5–10.

And the life everlasting
Revelation 21:1–22:5; 2 Peter 3:13.

Amen
Philippians 4:4–7, 11–13; Matthew 6:25–34;
19:16–22; John 12:26; Hebrews 13:5–6; 1 John
2:4–6; Psalm 56:10–11.

"Somehow
I'm left with
the feeling
I ought to
do something."